A Visit to

The Police Station

by Patricia J. Murphy

Consulting Editor: Gail Saunders-Smith, PhD

Reading Consultant: Jennifer Norford, Senior Consultant
Mid-continent Research for Education and Learning
Aurora, Colorado

Capstone
press

Mankato, Minnesota

T 5928

Pebble Plus is published by Capstone Press
151 Good Counsel Drive, P.O. Box 669, Mankato, Minnesota 56002
www.capstonepress.com

1 2 3 4 5 6 09 08 07 06 05 04

Library of Congress Cataloging-in-Publication Data
Murphy, Patricia J., 1963–
    The police station/by Patricia J. Murphy.
    p. cm.—(Pebble plus: A visit to)
    Includes bibliographical references and index.
    Contents: The police station—Police officers—Around the station—Glossary—Read More—Internet sites.
    ISBN 0-7368-2581-9 (hardcover)
    1. Police—Juvenile literature. 2. Police stations—Juvenile literature. [1. Police. 2. Police stations.] I. Title.
II. Series: A visit to (Mankato, Minn.)
HV7922.M87 2005
363.2—dc22   2003024961

Summary: Simple text and photographs present a visit to a police station.

Editorial Credits
Sarah L. Schuette, editor; Jennifer Bergstrom, series designer; Enoch Peterson, book designer; Karen Hieb,
    product planning editor

Photo Credits
Capstone Press/Gary Sundermeyer, front cover, 1, 5, 6–7, 8–9, 11, 12–13, 15, 17, 20–21
David R. Frazier Photolibrary, 19
PhotoDisc Inc./Siede Preis, back cover

Capstone Press thanks the North Mankato Police Department for its assistance with photo shoots.

Note to Parents and Teachers

The series A Visit to supports national social studies standards related to the production, distribution, and consumption of goods and services. This book describes and illustrates a visit to a police station. The images support early readers in understanding the text. The repetition of words and phrases helps early readers learn new words. This book also introduces early readers to subject-specific vocabulary words, which are defined in the Glossary section. Early readers may need assistance to read some words and to use the Table of Contents, Glossary, Read More, Internet Sites, and Index/Word List sections of the book.

Word Count: 115
Early-Intervention Level: 14

Table of Contents

The Police Station

A police station is a place where police officers work. Police officers help keep communities safe.

5

People report accidents
and crimes at the station.
They ask police officers
for help.

Dispatchers answer
emergency calls.
They send police officers
to help people.

Police Officers

Police officers check in
before starting their shifts.
The watch commander gives
them jobs at roll call.

Police officers drive squad cars. The cars have lights and sirens.

Some officers work with
dogs. The dogs help
officers investigate crimes.

Officers take fingerprints and mug shots. They interview suspects.

Around the Station

Police stations have cells.
Each cell has a bed,
a sink, and a toilet.

A police station is
busy day and night.
It is always open.

Glossary

cell—a small room with locks; some cells have bars.

dispatcher—a person who answers 911 calls and assigns rescue workers

interview—to ask questions about something important

investigate—to find out as much as possible about an event or a person

shift—a set number of hours that a person works

suspect—a person who may be responsible for a crime

Read More

Adamson, Heather. *A Day in the Life of a Police Officer.* Community Helpers at Work. Mankato, Minn.: Capstone Press, 2004.

Braithwaite, Jill. *Police Cars.* Pull Ahead Books. Minneapolis: Lerner, 2004.

Gordon, Sharon. *What's Inside a Police Station.* Bookworms. What's Inside? New York: Benchmark Books, 2003.

Internet Sites

FactHound offers a safe, fun way to find Internet sites related to this book. All of the sites on FactHound have been researched by our staff.

Here's how:

1. Visit *www.facthound.com*

2. Type in this special code **0736825819** for age-appropriate sites. Or enter a search word related to this book for a more general search.

3. Click on the **Fetch It** button.

FactHound will fetch the best sites for you!

Index/Word List